BOTTLED AIR

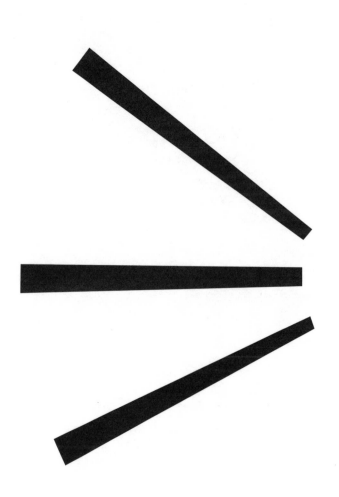

CALEB KLACES

BOTTLED AIR

EYEWEAR PUBLISHING

First published in 2013
by Eyewear Publishing Ltd
74 Leith Mansions, Grantully Road
London W9 1LJ
United Kingdom

Typeset with graphic design by Edwin Smet
Author photograph Oliver Smith
Printed in England by TJ International Ltd, Padstow, Cornwall

ISBN 978-1-908998-04-0

WWW.EYEWEARPUBLISHING.COM

**Caleb Klaces
is the 2012 winner of the Melita Hume Poetry Prize.
The winner received £1,000 and publication by Eyewear
Publishing. The 2012 Judge was Tim Dooley. His citation
read:**

'This is a powerful and original collection, which reveals its riches and depths gradually and rewards repeated reading. Klaces is well-read and does not wear his learning lightly, yet the poetry is not wilfully clever or self-satisfied but fully accessible – its engaging footnotes integrated into the wit and imagination of the whole work.

Bottled Air works as a book, not just a collection of poems. It evokes the tragic European past and the global instantaneous present. At its heart is a wounded compassion and an openness to the variousness of experience. What he writes in a poem set in a Bulgarian orphanage is true of much else in the book:
"... this is what being human is, really,
something plain and unbearably alive."
Klaces sets his own agenda as a writer but creates a trust
in the reader, which is unusually well rewarded.'

THE
MELITA HUME
POETRY PRIZE

Caleb Klaces
was born in Birmingham in 1983.
He is the author of the chapbook *All Safe All Well*
(Flarestack Poets, 2011), the winner of a 2012 Eric
Gregory Award, and a *Granta* New Poet.

Table of Contents

Notes — 72

Acknowledgements — 79

For Jo Klaces and David Draycott

Six Figurines

Set in and around a home for orphaned and mentally and physically disabled children in Bulgaria. Thanks to Joe and Sam.

Parachute

So now we are   in charge
     of the yard
OK everyone   got some parachute
     in their hands

You have hands   there
If you wouldn't mind
     please
be distracted   by us
     first
Here we go
Arms

     right up
     right up

so it explodes

So the
slow weight
     of the canvas

falls

Go on   under it
     Go on
     into the dark

Come out   come out
Please
     come out

Our turn

to disappear

Cat

Children, halved, backing into a chalky wall,
intent, intense, grammatical:
an opening, closing row of cat flaps.

Sunlight fusses on flies, fades primary colours.
Then a real cat arrives from the grass,
and one bell, then another, and all over one another,

cries as children's legs straighten, walk children
towards that slanted body gone.
That tail leads heads into one another

and yellow flies. Around
and around until heads are dizzy and legs
feel their distant weight, the ground, back

backing into a chalky wall,
intent, intense, grammatical:
an opening, closing row of cat flaps.

Sob

       The girl with all those breasts
through her loose faded T-shirt
       never seems to want to
be doing what passionately
       she is kissing Sam's arm
leg hooked around his leg and then
       biting so he holds her
firmly off and she turns runs
       ahead of herself to
just far enough over there
       to fold down on the grass
into one altogether sob.

Music

One afternoon we had them doing papier mâché. Bowls of flour and water and piles of shredded newspaper were laid out across the table. We had spent the break time getting dizzy blowing up balloons, so each child had one to cover in newspaper and paste. When the mixture was dry, the balloons could be popped to leave a hard shell. We didn't know what we'd do with the shells. The room smelled like rising bread. Half-plastered balloons began bouncing around, twisting under uneven weight.

A nurse wheeled in a girl we had not met before. Her large head was tilted forward and her back slightly arched in her chair. When her eyes flickered open, they were gluey white. She doesn't see and doesn't speak, they said. She is from another country and nobody here knows her language. There she sat. After a while, Joe decided he would do something. He filled a toilet roll tube with beads and sealed the ends. He curled her fingers around the instrument and shook it in both of their hands to make a sound. When he took away his hand the instrument fell onto her lap. He picked it up and placed it back in her grip. This time it stayed. We waited for her to shake it. Meanwhile, the rest of the room swelled.

The nurses had told us classical music was calming for them. Let's do that. Yes, this is what they want. This is great. Piano smoothing everything out, slowing everyone down. Everything all of a piece now. Voices folding into the music, making a sort-of meaning. It doesn't matter what meaning. Look, she is with us now, together in the music. A different dizziness. All safe. All well. All light. If you popped us you'd be left with a single, immaculate shell of light. Please turn it off, the nurse says, the children are getting upset.

Her

It was a relief to share the secret
until it turned out all three of us
had been keeping it. We couldn't bear
to be around the blank boy
who was, remember, a girl, we shook
our heads and drank from cold, cheap beers,
as if it was a particular shame
we had to remember that for her.
And was it, if we were honest—honesty
we'd decided was important—
something like spite
that made her only click and growl?
Didn't she want to speak?
She looked like she would cry or laugh forever,
if her slanted mouth could ever agree
on its accusation. Too lost.
Wrong in the wrong ways. The dream
where nothing much happens,
that doesn't need even to be shooed
from the bedside. But here
it is again, here I am again,
as a growl, a click, a stare, the lucid fear
of concluding this is what being human is, really,
something plain and unbearably alive.
By the time we had found our hotel,
the answer had marched triumphantly through the streets
but lost its nerve
and dispersed finally
at the palace gates.

In the morning, she was us,
but not the basic us, not an us
we have tamed. There is no monster
within. There is another kind of
answer. Much easier to love
and dislike the other girl, who was angry

and pinched and stole and banged her fists on the cold floor;
much easier to forgive the funny boy
who shat himself laughing and laughed some more.

Favourite

Somebody left the gate open.

They are stealing old toast from a skip in the other field.
Some have fists of clear plastic to crackle and own.

We chase them back.
It's like getting bees into jars,

all scattering except Pilet, his little yellow head
hung over the pile of rubbish like a dab of paint.

Inside his head is a yellow chick,
growing, otiose, and growing.

Every so often something attempts to take off in his throat,
or he walks, above the ground,

a smile always with him in its grip.

Beginning Again

Elegy, for Celia

The second time it became extinct, the Pyrenean ibex
        lasted seven minutes: a weak-lunged clone
        grown in a goat, rotten copy of 'Celia',
        who went the first time under a falling tree.
I don't know how to have lost what
        comes
back, what we should say for the passed
        that we repeat
        like a word revived to be the name
        of a yacht or a drink.

I spent an afternoon coppicing in a small, still wood
agitated by roads
        with those lovely despairing grey-haired women who
        have come on their own
to cut brambles back or walk the course
of dried-up rivers, who feel the other world
falling away, picking needles
        from the canal. Who replant,
        who still sign petitions,
so otters are common beside farmland again,
some road construction delayed.
They drank elderflower cordial and I left my Sprite unopened
        in my bag
        until I got home.

What has been lost and what gained not
        a possible sum. Before
        the anthropocene: an aggregate of
        failures, unauthored revisions in search of
        uses, so *variety always better*
than dullness is the best I can keep caring
        about deletions with, which
I
        do.
Same sickly Celias scattered across the crags
        mingling with goats seems
        less dull than them nowhere
        at all.

The women remind the larvae in the bark
        of their Latin name
        as they chop willow to the base to grow
again, as if
something named
        will live
        regardless
        of them.

Cheering the relief boat

I

The boat is not in the bay. Marston and Hurley are shelling limpets.
The seals are in the bay. Penguins slip from white rocks.
Marston heaves in his greasy furs, aiming a shell at the horizon.
Hoosh boils in the hut. Black smoke hangs in the air.
Limpets clamp. Marston weeps in hoosh smoke. The sea slaps itself.
The tears loosen the bay. A football is in the air. Furs are loosened.
Men aim with their insoles. Toes are white rocks. Lungs clamp.
Hoosh hangs in the lungs. Marston hears the sea slap the boat.
Marston cuts toward the boat in the bay. Shouts hang in the air.
Spray shines Marston's skin. Marston is in the sea. Seals shine the rocks.
The horizon blackens. Marston is going. Shouts slip off white rocks.
The sea clamps bone. Icy feet line the shore. The boat is not in the bay.
The horizon shouts. Hurley boils. The sea weeps Marston ashore.
Hurley clamps Marston. Marston heaves. Feet disperse.
Hot hoosh shines Marston's iced lungs in the hut.
Bones whiten in skin. Seals aim the football around the rocks.
Penguins blacken the horizon. The boat is not in the bay. Limpets clamp.

II

About a year ago I went to an exhibition at the Royal Geographical Society in London, of Frank Hurley's photographs from the 1914-17 Trans-Antarctic expedition led by Ernest Shackleton. Following the destruction of his ship, Shackleton left most of his crew stranded on Elephant Island, in the hope that he would return with a vessel big enough to transport them all. On the day of Shackleton's departure for South Georgia, a tiny island in the South Atlantic, Hurley set up his camera on the shore and took a photograph from behind the men, waving across the bay to the boat headed for the horizon. Four months and almost two thousand nautical miles later, Shackleton did return, and Hurley later altered his image so that it became *Cheering the Relief Boat,* a portrait of rescue. Nobody knows why. Struck by the image (also referred to as *All Safe, All Well*, as all 22 men still on Elephant Island had managed to stay both alive and sane), the alteration of which was not entirely successful, leaving a black scar around the boat in the bay, I bought a postcard and left, walking along Exhibition Rd and onto Kensington Road to the bus stop for the number 10. The only other person at the stop was a woman in her mid-thirties who, once I'd taken my headphones off, told me that she was going to throw herself into the road in front of the double-decker. Rather than talk her out of it, or wait and see, I turned around, walked away and didn't look back. In my memory, she is always mid-jump, neither alive nor dead.

A nothing to do with God

1996, at the bus stop, my friend, mouth brown with Marmite
          and the paler brown of nicotine,
dressed up for the last, non-uniform, day of term
          in a Kappa tracksuit brought back from Zante,
electric blue with silver trim, asked hadn't my dad once
          been a pope or something?

        ★

I liked the idea of the Sistine Chapel, that it had been larger
          than Michelangelo's life. Larger than
a football pitch. Too large to take in? I asked my father,
          wanting him to nod his head solemnly.
It's still a general rule, that things should be larger
          than they are here, him older then

than he is now. And what an idea
          that a day could be *ruined*. The morning was still
as it had been before I kicked my sister
          under the train table coming home
from the old bombed Coventry Cathedral. In the new one

          there is a photograph of two charred beams
that fell in such a way as to resemble a crucifix.
          And there is the crucifix hung on the wall
like one charred beam fallen on another.

          My father said nothing to do with God
but looked intently towards nothing in particular
          above the altar as he gave us coins
to drop in the model of the cathedral
          inside the cathedral.

        ★

Not yet thirty and already a star, Andreas Vesalius
       renounced the study of anatomy.
No longer should I willingly spend long hours
       in the Cemetery of the Innocents
turning over bones, nor to Montfaucon to look at bones.
       Nor should I care to be locked out of Louvain
so that I might take away bones from the gibbet.

       But he could not entirely stop
and never failed to visit any nearby medical school,
       nor to inspect the bodies on the battlefield.

         ★

My father hitch-hiked to Israel in 1960
       and took notes. As the train pulled out
of the station, he realised that his bag was gone.
       Would he still have become a priest,
and then not one, he asks me, if he had returned
       from Israel and Naples and Belgrade
with his notebooks—if he had
       had, after repatriation from Rotterdam
by boat, his own account of himself?

         ★

       Bound for Venice, after his trip
to the Holy Land, the reasons for which are lost,
       in 1564, a storm took apart his boat
and with its remains Vesalius was washed up on Zakynthos,
       the island on which the tar was dredged
that failed to protect the ship, and which is known now
       by British tourists as Zante.

Where precisely he landed is not known, nor do we know
       where he was buried, by whom.
There seems little doubt, at least,
       that this was in the month of October.

Painting over Aya Sofia

A lot of the painting here is painting over.
Can everyone at the back hear over everyone?
Everyone is a blast of light seeping across the film.
All day high toothy windows whiten in flashlight.

We are much like we were: five times a day.
Things don't change that much in five centuries.
For ten centuries before it was faces.
Those were faces, yes. They were angels.

The gold mosaic is as fine as an angel's wing.
The Christian building is spongy yellow, ochre, gold.
The Islamic additions are sheer yellow, baby blue, black and gold.
Red crosses seep through baby blue.

A woman kisses her cross and crosses herself.
Another is kissed by a pink polo shirt and camera.
A camera will not put the rest of Christ back in.
It will not take away the crowd around Christ's toes.

The crowded reference image accompanying the fragments.
Pigeons wing through the high windows and up in fragments.
Christ's toes; Christ's fingertips; Christ's thigh; Christ on high.
Sandals expose toes in the highlights.

My line

III

And here I am crying, which I never do,
because they loved one another across all that time

with no hope of love back, except the kind not directed at them
but at something more precise: the golden bees,

which in this context is easier than saying *Dad*.
Because. Because right here in this line is where

he has always lived and I have been a visitor
sharing tea, and he is showing me a photograph

of a man's aura and I am saying, 'Yes, but I think
it must be something to do with the light.'

II

But being is already being again, Browne wrote, which I like more
now that it is out of context, being being other people again,

my father, excited to show me a photograph in which he had
unwittingly captured the aura of a jogger in the park,

ashy smudge around the man's body, was laughed at,
is how I imagine it is written in the entry for the day, kept

with all his diaries in the Birmingham Central Library
because the friendly archivist was convinced

that the record of this curate turned poet could be history
given the chance. 'The details are there in the archive,' says my father

more often now no longer remembering what the year was,
or why exactly, or who, 'but I didn't just read about it.'

I

In the three centuries between when the strange three hundred
golden bees found in Childeric's tomb were described

in *Urne Buriall* and then *The Rings of Saturn*, they had passed
from Belgium to the Netherlands, Austria and on to France,

where they were kept in an obscure room of the then Bibliothèque Royale
until they were stolen. There were only two found, in leather sacks

in the Seine, by the time Jorge Luis Borges wrote that he was
revising an uncertain Quevidian translation of *Urn Burial*,

which he was, and W.G. Sebald wasn't, when he slid
Borges' imagined Borges almost unchanged into German

and under the name he had taken to write with after emigrating
first to Manchester and then settling in East Anglia,

where the urns were unexpectedly found that prompted Browne,
in 1658, to remark on the barbarous magnificence of the sepulchral obsequies

of Childeric's time, and how very little we know of what people
really leave with, which seems most likely to be nothing.

Over Amazonia

The office crowded around my screen
to see new people aiming bows and arrows
up at us.
Bald spot in uncut cover,
like a bird's-eye view of my father.
Drawn out from under thatched *malocas*
by noisy glass and steel—from Italy,
Belgium, Russia, China...—
people painted black and red
attack God.
God eats them like Pac-man.
They light a fire in Pac-man's lungs.

Over here

When the noxious reservoir
cracked and villages were allowed to be red,
kitchens and dogs allowed, and the river
and the man who could not find his
mother,
        who loaded every stuck bicycle
            onto his truck to wait together
for as long as they were useless;
                when reporters
politely nibbled freshly baked cakes
listening to little lost red children;
        when the red cortèges hurried
            through the streets;
when the bulldozers rearranged
ruined fields
        into an emergency dam,
she was
        picking up sticks
            on the beach, standing
them up into emergency rhyme
        and remembering something
she had read in the news
about sand from one coastline
        being sold to increase another.

In protest, the swimming crab fishermen
        were allowed to smash the dredgers,
            once, twice.
She was with them,
but over here:
not allowed to be
caught.

Every room built on the relocated sand
        has the same view of the island.
It's printed on the windows,
            along with the birds
    she allowed not to land.

Sky, after all, meets nothing

OK Texas.
From the horizon
a long withdrawing gold to black slick to
the rental car sifting pearly butterflies
as it rolls
into the distance always appearing
to slide under hopeful uprights
of ownership,
fence posts and pylons
all in mid-
fall,
the carpet slowly pulled.

The car is a closed system of water bottles, trail mix, maps
and an audiobook *History of Modern Britain* we say we should
stop listening to
but don't, so quiet Clement Attlee takes his place
among the invisible elements:
pollen, white pine blister, spruce aphid
running the borders in plain sight
of the immigration authority blimp.
It's the only thing
in the sky,
pin
in the map.

At a diner

            we get going with a proud-jawed

insurance man disappointed

            with Texas, he says, without

explanation, but instead straight into

            where are you from with those accents,

and then

            the boat—*your* boat—only so large:

                as more and more people get in,

the sickest are thrown overboard.

                And for the first time I think

I understand how taxes might feel like

            strapping your dollars to a pigeon

and sending it off across the burning ridge

            in the direction of DC

with no hope of return

            if you live with this kind of distance.

We are not sure how to dislike people we meet
while we are visitors.

Dusk brings on a singalong,
                              reflections
                in the windows,
                        hush.

At Big Bend, Mark the bird expert warns us not to trust the colours
in our field guides
because artists feel compelled,
he has come to believe,
to brighten and enhance the duller birds.

        From my notebook:
                the crow a blackest rip in the grainy blue.

At least we can all agree that black vultures
                        are big
                                at any height.
                                        And when more vultures
glide out on stiff, thick wings
                from the rocks,
                        it is not the birds that appear
to diminish
        but the sky.

Cats on Fire

A postcard that fell from a book about writing books
      of history
      bent double a beautiful man
      who handing it back to me said,
      'Here's one for you:
      as a child I had no reason
      not to believe my mother
      when she claimed it was she
      alone could ignite the flames
      inside the cat's eyes
      that with faultless timing
      unblinded the country lanes
      we rolled dimly through
      from swimming practice home.'

Google retrieved: a bad band's mp3s;
        videos of cats on fire,
        of a cat being thrown through a window
        on fire; photographs of angry-looking cats
        doctored to make them look
        like they are angry
        because they are on fire;
        and somewhere down the second page
        a passage from Sir James George Frazer's *Golden Bough*,
        in which he writes,
        'In the department of the Ardennes cats were flung
        into the bonfires kindled on the first Sunday in Lent;
        sometimes, by a refinement of cruelty,
        they were hung over the fire
        from the end of a pole and roasted alive.'
        As late
        as the seventeenth-century,
        Parisians collected the embers and ashes
        of the cats
        and took them home,
        believing or not
        that they would bring good luck.

The night before we met courtesy of the postcard, the man
        had been tired,
        curled around his laptop
        on the floor,
        with a bottle of warm beer
        and photographs
        from a holiday in Poland.
        Declining the offer
        of plum brandy
        from the man dragged kicking
        by his own smile out
        of the woods each afternoon.
        Cool in the stream.
        China cats
        in the ex-pat's cottage,
        with a funny line embroidered
        and pinned to the wall:
        'The only thing a cat has to fear
        is fur itself'.

The author of the book, a Polish reporter, one evening
  on a balcony
  in Dar es Salaam,
  drained by hungry mosquitoes,
  copied into his notebook
  a passage from *The Histories* by Herodotus,
  who had heard
  that when a house is on fire
  the Egyptians don't run for water
  but position themselves at intervals around it
  to get in the way of the cats
  that slip between them,
  jump over them even,
  to dash into the fire.
  The reporter was shocked.
  There had been no cats in *The Histories* before.
  One must open great books again,
  he remembers,
  if one is to catch
  falling from between their pages
  their hidden cats
  dashing into their hidden fires.

The librarian held a book between the trolley and the shelf
     as the man went on,
     'I imagined cats buried
     up to their eyes
     in the tarmac. With each
     burble of the wheels
     I dug my nails deeper
     into my arm.
     Of course I didn't believe
     cats were really
     entombed.
     But the dry sting
     of chlorine will always
     bring to mind
     the cracked heads
     of hidden cats
     and my arm in red and blue.'

On the postcard was a black-and-white photograph
        of sorry houses
        of tarpaulin and string
        and corrugated iron
        on the slide of a hill.
        It was beautiful too,
        but difficult
        to enjoy,
        so when we got home
        I slipped it
        behind a framed photograph
        in which it looks like
        I am cupping the Taj Mahal
        in my hand
        for safe-keeping.

A thin Polish cat's clumsy young were close enough
for her to sleep
on the bank rising
to the cottage.
'I lay there naked
with her,' he said,
wagging my penis
like it was
a teacher's finger.
According to Herodotus,
when the female cats of Egypt
are distracted by their young
from the habit
of going to the males,
the males
remove the kittens secretly
or by force.
It is a creature extremely fond
of its young
and must replace them.
'What else to do
but return to
your bloody mate?'

When the Ardennes cats burned in burning wicker cages,
        their screams were accompanied
        by boiling skin's syncopated popping
        and the crowd was delighted
        to be rid of witches.
        When a cat died a natural death
        in ancient Egypt
        the people of its household
        would shave off their eyebrows
        in mourning. When
        I fell asleep that night I had a dream.
        In the dream, there was a fire.
        Through a door in the fire
        was a country lane.
        In the middle of the lane,
        an envelope. On the envelope:
        'For the present',
        and in smaller letters below:
        'No cheating'.
        I opened it
        and there was the beautiful man
        in a frame. I had the feeling
        I was being unfaithful
        to him
        with him
        but he assured me the water he swam in
        would protect my house
        from fire.
        I didn't believe it
        but hung it on a nail
        above the door
        anyway.

When the following morning we were woken by each other,
>>the man reported
>>he had not been able to sleep
>>in a stranger's bed.
>>He had tried a modern kind
>>of counting sheep,
>>clicking one-by-one
>>through Google images,
>>looking for, but not
>>hoping to find,
>>the postcard's slums.
>>Instead,
>>he said,
>>he had come across a poem
>>called 'Hot Demolition'
>>that had a sickening footnote:
>>'This term refers to the contemporary practice
>>of some Filipino landlords
>>who will douse a cat with kerosene,
>>set it alight, then direct it
>>into tindery shanties.
>>It is a cheap way of clearing the land,
>>which can then be relet.'
>>He said he didn't really need
>>to read the poem
>>after that.

When later in the morning we trotted arm-in-arm
        through the shopping centre,
        we got some looks.
        He thought he heard
        a group of women spill
        something about being
        put to the stake.
        'That's Birmingham for you,'
        I said, rolling my eyes, but
        was scared and started
        talking any old rubbish.
        'You know how *cat*
        means girlfriend...
        and a *cat on fire*
        is a hard-on
        in need of
        attention...well
        they can't both be cats,
        can they,
        let alone on fire,
        when one is inside
        the other?!' He laughed
        but said nothing
        for a while.

As far as I can see, there are two basic flame-types.
>Nasty slight quick
>ones grasping
>everything they can
>and slow
>lush choosy ones
>so cool they look
>thirst-quenching.
>Does fire look
>the same
>everywhere?
>What if you are Polish
>and in Africa?

Before his 'first moult', he eventually replied, he avoided
    anyone he suspected
    of being a fairy.
    When once a friend was
    masturbating,
    proposing,
    he joined
    because he knew
    then the friend
    could not really
    want him
    like that.
    'I saw some photos
    the other day,' he sighed, raising
    his chin
    for a dramatic pause,
    'turns out he's a great big bear.'

When we had said goodbye, him not kissing back as much
          as I was kissing, but
          promising to message
          soon,
          I wanted to write the poem
          the man had not been able
          to bring himself
          to read
          in my bed,
          without bringing myself
          to read it either.
          It seemed romantic to remember
          for both of us
          what neither of us
          had seen.
          I reopened
          the book by the Polish reporter
          but nothing fell out.
          I would have to begin
          on my own
          with embers,
          the same
          if the fire started
          in an accident
          during kerosene-lit work
          to pay for the children's school uniforms
          and if it started
          with a cat
          running away
          from its fur ablaze.

16 Airs

Manila: Thousands of people made homeless after a spectacular fire ripped through a crowded shanty town in the Philippine capital queued for food on Monday as they pondered how to rebuild their lives ...One man who escaped the fire but went back in to retrieve his air conditioner was the only person confirmed to have been killed.

—Associated Press

★

The whole strangely recalled fancy pictures of troglodyte dwellings of anchorites such as I remembered having seen long, long ago in the early Italian paintings. Perhaps it was this reminiscence, or the unconscious vision of rich rubbish deposits which such holy cave-dwellers might have left behind in the burrows, that made me in my mind people these recesses with a beehive of Buddhist monks, and wonder what awkward climbs they might have had when paying each other visits.

—Sir Aurel Stein, on first visiting the Mogao Caves, North West China

★

What sort of breathing space is most conducive to civilised life[?]

—Bruno Latour

Flight

Under the watery throttle of screens, tannoy and neon shopfronts,
    which squeezes out anything grown and anything unpredictable,
the hull buried in your chest was already difficult to pull back,
    like one of those steel-plated lines that sink with waking up.

A group of excited men splashed around immovable seats.
    I could have won you a sports car. I could have bought you a large watch.
Struggling, I imagined the organs inside your hull
    and thought of them as poised and fitting together perfectly;

mine, I thought, are probably slightly squashing one another.
    By the time I was in the air it did not feel crass to think that
life is meaningless, which even in Departures was embarrassing.
    In the clouds you were called in as meaning; the boat just

appearing. Not organs any more but an idea of connection.
    We are alive and will be dead. I could have bought you a large watch,
for all the waiting you do, which mostly, I hope, does not feel
    like waiting, but when it does I would like to recognise it,

as an enthusiast who, when it really starts to pour with rain,
    stops digging up his garden and comes inside to sit with tea
and look through the window at the wet earth and scattered peonies,
    seeing only what patient lives must float underneath.

The cave is woken up

Waking cut into manageable pieces
       by the snooze button. The Great Wall's
lookout towers, built at regular intervals, seem
       at once to cosy up to one another and,
respectfully, to give some distance. Phone locates
       itself. There's no way that was eight minutes.

'Are you asleep?' she asks on the phone.
       Which side are we supposed to be guarding
again? The view, I think,
       between alarms.
'Superficial', she replies, 'dregs
       left in the bottom of the cup;
the tea is what is important.' She
       is always finding secret caves
in metaphors.
           Beyond the western reaches of the Wall,
       one of hundreds carved into a cliff
was stuffed with sacred manuscripts
       and sealed for almost a millennium.

'What time is it with you?'

       At the turn of the twentieth-century,
the monk appointed by himself caretaker
       of the sacred rubbish was persuaded
by Aurel Stein that the explorer should be able
       to load up his ponies and
'Don't miss me too much today'

       two years later the cave was empty.

A whale full of books

Having, for the first time, been, himself, in a whale,
       a *Physeter macrocephalus*, or sperm, washed up
on the Norfolk coast, noisy with jealous seagulls
       and making an abominable scent, Browne imagines
the ancient land of the fish-eaters,
       where the architecture was all hung
from the skeletons of whales.
       What would cities of Jonahs
have been like? Imagine the woman
       going out of her mind with what
had happened below her on the rocks
       as she leant helplessly into the wind—
a hundred refugees down there drowned—
       passing through a whale's jaw
to her physician. Imagine the long, grey ribs
       they walk under in the herb garden,
sharing what she has seen.
       Imagine the deep bone in which
the herbs are ground. We now see
       all this apparatus better than the fish-eaters,
I would guess, wrote a largely forgotten
       book collector—rich, in the end,
from the bottling of air—it being only normal
       for them, and thus, as forgotten
as the ring I gave you
       when we were children.
The husband had grown isolated
       and afraid of his books.
He encased the volume he had most loved
       in what he was told were bits of that ship
broken on those rocks of that new land.
       The point is no longer to read the horrific thing,
he would write in letters to his wife,
       but absorb its poisonous ink.
Like the Polynesian gods, he wrote, which I
       have visited many times

in the British Museum, my book
        requires a new casing placed almost monthly
on top of the last. Anything unwrapped
        comes to loom over me like an impossible
father. Every week now, more bits
        of broken ships. If you can find more,
my little bird, I am always
        in need of those pieces
that have survived. Soon it will be bigger
        than the house,
which I am selling. I am selling
        that Uccello painting, the one,
as Schwob writes, do you remember,
        in which somewhere in the battle
you can clearly see the shape
        of his wife. He didn't notice
she was dead, as he had not, as you know,
        noticed she was alive,
but her pale blue shape
        appears amongst all the others
he had gathered about him
        on his island, married
to strange sounds,
        boats, whalebones, the books
he would not drown.

A sense of space

We were clever with the conservatory, hardly had to take away
        a brick, nothing demolished, just moved
the existing wall, knocked a window through, brought the lawn in
        two or three feet. I'll admit I might have exaggerated
how cramped a condition we were living in
        to convince myself of the necessity of an extension.
Or maybe every space does have a natural lifespan. When it dies
        inside we have a duty to dispose of the remains
and make something new. But how to be sure
        when it has passed? That occurred to me listening
to Full Fathom Five set to a minimal techno vibe
        in the underwater glass tunnel at the Sea Life Centre.
It was like crawling through the corpse of the words.
        Alternatively, I thought: pour salt into your Evian
and imagine you are drowning. Afterwards,
        we went and stupidly bought a load of flat-packed space
on special offer. When we realised the cost of the air
        to go with it, the feeling reminded me of hugging
my grandmother too hard, after which she took to her bed
        for a month of rest and spiteful text messages.
By the way, Marie left just before you arrived.
        She went looking for food. She pays for it with her trick,
which is to say everything backwards. 'Little girl,'
        the men shout, 'come over here. Come here
and I'll give you a plum if you sing me a song to the beginning.'

The husband and the rest of the world

Envelopes of middle-age I send off
to the old; wasted energy to the dead.
Everything important I forget goes out
with the recycling each Thursday
and, to stimulate exchange
I ship in my air from nowhere, China.
The boat goes back
full of British sense of humour,
so no carbon is emitted
for nothing.

I have heard
people sell body parts
to get on the boat.
One of the refugees (not *refugees*,
a spokesperson is careful to point out,
displaced persons. Well, most of them,
some of them just persons
and a few waiting for approval on that.
We think a small minority
may have made themselves up
so they have something to escape with)
borrows my avatar. He sells his teeth
on SilkRoad.com.
I use the profit to buy him time.

Meanwhile, indoors, in spring

Slept through a storm.
  The wet garden
an impatiently opened envelope,
    bristling. Laughter in the bedroom,
which on inspection I decided
    was me.

I came late to the seasons.
    It's the first spring
I've ever noticed: unpaid swallows
    doting on the football pitch.
Every year creeping around the same?
    Out there? What else
have I missed? What else
    has survived centuries of praise
only to have the glass doors swish closed
    in its face?
      The forgetting of hot
in cold as you step inside
    the air-conditioned shopping centre.
Relief that tastes like cappuccino.
    Feel free to borrow our air
while you browse.

Explaining our habitats

She grew up in the countryside
        and hates golf courses.
Their neatness, she wrote, stops history.
        So here: a photograph
of a fairway—mown smooth as plastic wrap
        over a landfill—which had turned
slowly grey-brown then collapsed
        to reveal a pit of rusted signs and black liquid.

I played golf once and liked,
        as the hole finally took the ball,
the feeling of having got a tiny future
        right. By the time

it arrived, she had told me
        everything in her letter
except the letter, the envelope,
        the grubbiness of transit
between then and now. Of
        welcoming a stranger home.

It is spring here,
        if you can imagine. Wasps
are explaining perspective
        from the head of a nail.
Some cells stay closed, bodies
        under wings,
or never wings, never bodies—
        never formatted
            for today's brief purpose.
               More purpose to go around
               for us?

How they had kept one another

On the last day we took off our clothes
          and ran around the university
in the tradition of making an exception.
          Then for the final hours
we lay together, love's familiars,
          before ourselves, whilst outside
the shade came to prop up the oaks.
          That city, as far as we knew,
without a slum, was under-the-top.
          'I am poor because
something I did in a previous life
          was bad enough
the punishment overflowed
          into this one,' said Marie.
It is necessary for some people to be unnecessary,
          she had written on a scrap of paper
pinned between a broken fan
          and a photograph of a bird.
Stein describes his first day
          at the Caves of The Thousand Buddhas
as one of *over-abundant sight-seeing*
          that repeats on his mind's eye
throughout the night. Too much the only way
          to enough. Us, nothing
will ever satisfy us
          that we can't unwrap down to nothing
but seed-husks, Styrofoam
          and down there; love just passing
hotly through, as it passes through
          the tunnels of a cigarette.
All you need to be happy is happiness inside,
          my arse. Not enough;
too much. One day
          the treat will be the filter
and the sea will be housed inside the whale
          inside the Sea Life Centre.

The cursor and other freedoms

As long as nothing has yet been logged into
        there is grace. A little fluorescent blob of it.
But my card, gentlemen, is full. Once online I shall dance all night,
        an impatient waltz, in which the third beat
is always skipped. Too eager am I to know another page
        for the first time. Besides,
these pop-ups are increasingly difficult to subdue.
        And I must take good care of my shadow,
lest others do. We move from room to painted room,
        the cave library, the whale's head—

we make our visit. We rehearse. When will we stop
        rehearsing? The small dark club
contains the universe, until the morning when its face gets so
        accusatory. Still, it asks no questions
and is answered by the blackened feet that stumble out
        and thicken on the airy street.

I'm sorry, I seem to have forgotten your name.
        Can you remember what you said it was?
Everyone is playing and I am not.
        I am playing and no-one else is. A dancer

has stopped to take a drink of water
        just off-screen. The cursor runs out of its medium.

The swallow, another freedom, wings it.

Vapours

'I think you are feeling lucky this evening?' he says,
        waving a packet of glow-in-the-dark
condoms at me, as he had when I'd slapped
        his back an hour ago, like we were
getting to know one another, 'So where are you from?'
        which got a spray of eau de cologne,
'Now the young ladies won't be able to control themselves',
        and I checked in the mirror, fingers
in the mint imperials, him turned and waving
        to a man in stride, who pinned him against
the tiles, spitting blood, 'You fucked
        my night, that knock-off piss you doused
my neck with set my skin on fire',
        friends pulling him off and the scuffle
shattering fluorescent bulbs over
        the slip and shove through the door,
so out under the dance floor's UV
        we glowed like an exclusive club,
which I hoped wasn't some reality
        TV setup, but more benign natural philosopher's
inquiry, like whether the glow-worm's dance
        is essential to its glow, keeping
under a bell jar specimens that *declined*
        and their luminous humour dried
until it was extinguished with their bodies,
        observed the same gentle Dr Browne,
who, to the Norwich court hearing the case
        of two ugly old women accused
of invisibly inciting two young girls
        to vomit needles and nails, of vanishing
a firkin of herrings, and other witchery,
        said that the Devil had surely played His part
to stir up and excite the humours of the children's
        bodies, and the witches were hanged,
the last almost in England, although how much
        we should attribute this to Browne's testimony

and how we should judge him, depends, it seems,
        on our impression of the jury's
susceptibility to the glow of a little fame,
        and if one believes the best part of a life
vouches for the rest: perhaps on that day
        the doctor had an excess of choler;
or perhaps nobody should be judged
        by the habitual cruelties of their age;
and perhaps the man selling vapours
        in the toilets had it coming, most
likely slipping watches from drunken wrists
        while stinging them with watery lavender
and citrus, and perhaps it's a relief to find
        that when that fluorescent toilet light
goes out each night he is completely sublimed,
        so to love and to hate him is only
to love and to hate the impure atmosphere.

His wife replies practically

Please don't sell the house.
　　　It is full of things—of you,
your books,
　　　what about the pelicans,
the boxes of flies in the attic,
　　　the seafowl you have kept alive
in the bathtub for so long?
　　　Everything I read about
in your letters. Besides,
　　　there is bound to be plague here
again soon and the whole lot
　　　put to the fire. Sorry,
what an unhelpful thing to write.
　　　But I hate to amend myself.
If we cannot live together
　　　we must at least be plain
with the run of our minds.
　　　I don't feel intimidated anymore—
it is what I love about you.
　　　Yes, I remember the painting,
it is quite ugly, as is, from
　　　the sound of it, its painter.
Get what you can
　　　and invest it in the business of air.
A little piece of everything that's ever lived—
　　　that should be your slogan...

The sun in a box

When I was younger I drafted a memory.
      I drew a rectangle on a piece of card
and called it a computer. Happy hours
      spent playing with framed nothing,
imagining a game I had seen in the Argos catalogue,
      only with me inserted into it
alongside the ghostcatcher, catching ghosts.
      What would you need to construct spring?
The Japanese do indoor summer
      at the indoor beach. Through the window
yesterday I saw a slow heron with a crow
      holding on to its outstretched leg,
which now feels indispensable
      as the cavity wall insulation
that has already saved enough on heating
      for two weeks' holiday this year.
The installation man's Polish apprentice
      pumped it into the wall
without checking for holes, and when the wall
      wasn't full after a good quarter
of an hour, he opened the kitchen door
      to find it bursting with
hot white foam. 'Like the sun
      in a box,' he said. I told him
he should have posted it online,
      now those eagle chicks have fled
the shot.
      After a week, a felt-tip crack
appeared on the screen
      where I'd dropped it.

Speaking of which

I used to believe that families lived inside the Berlin Wall,
          which I assumed to be as thick as my house
and hollowed out like a baguette. Nobody noticed *that*
          until I had eaten the evidence,
but where would the rubble have gone? Where
          does it ever go? Space seems to have
plenty of space. But it is a kind of idea, out there.
          Here, things are so heartbreakingly material.
On the steps of the Blue Mosque
          someone hands out little blue plastic bags to snap
over visitors' shoes. That the means we have of being holy
          crackles on the soft carpet
like a baby's nappy. That the money for the funeral
          comes from a loud day of playing cards
in the same cemetery where everyone lives.
          The girl who sleeps between corrugated iron
and cloth on graves stacked three high is glad
          of the bodies. Up there, it is easier to breathe,
a little further from the plastic bags and plastic bags
          of excreta. That the waste products
of holiness end up where people live and die
          and are holy. With my clean-air, clean-
conscience fortune, I took her out on a sled. 'Marie,'
          I said, 'Marie, this is snow, this is falling
for fun.'

The glass door

I haven't turned the computer on today
        to see how my life is doing
but breakfast was a success. I opened all the windows
        and all the doors
to let in the air. John Donne believed,
        I think he really believed,
that angels were air and wore air, wore
        it down upwards towards
their impossible purity. Then
        a friend emailed saying angels
no longer believe they are real.
        No feather stirs, no dust,
no other air imprints the air—'let him
        teach me that nothing',
goes a different poem. I thought it was
        the right question.
Two days looking for nothing
        until I bounced my head off the glass door
of being loved. Me and Skype know
        how excessive are
real people. How over-the-top
        what is
is, and you much too replete
        in real time
to warrant. 'I'
        lags. 'You'
lags.
        'Love lovely glorious'
lags
        and the air is full of hats
recording the wind as the priest,
        eyes down, reads his fond
exaggerated phrases to a field
        of giggling.

Emigrants deface the caves

After the British, the French and the Russian collectors,
       more Russians made it to the Mogao caves,
emigrants sent there by Chinese bureaucrats
       who didn't know what else to do with them.
They had left together because they were unwanted
       not because they were friends;
half had stopped talking to the other half,
       who slept in the upper caves, in shifts.
In one cave a smiling statue is dressed in robes
       painted with pictures of rooms
in which men sit cross-legged facing statues
       dressed in men-in-rooms pattern,
the surface repeated, revealed,
       inside itself and so on like gossip.
The emigrants wrote their names all over the statue,
       carved genitals into its mouth
and cut out its eyes. 'The kind of thing people do
       to find out where they are,'
my friend would say after biting his wife
       in his sleep. 'In my dream I was in a house
with no walls,' he'd tell me, out getting his bearings,
       in an open space, on his own.
He once woke under a desk
       on the eighteenth floor of an empty office block.
The panicked guard sat him down
       in front of the security tapes
and they had silently watched nothing happen
       in silent grey rooms for an hour
by the time my friend saw himself
       slip through the back door.
Nobody had ever seen the cave behind the water.
       'Please don't show it in your film,'

requested the elder tribesman. 'We would rather not pry
　　　　where the swifts go. It is their place,
not ours.' The elder and the director shook hands.
　　　　They understood one another.
But how could he not take a camera
　　　　through the falls, just once, to turn
on himself, to star in what wasn't really there?

Beginning again

Stepped out of our mirrors for a first clumsy kiss
      in Arrivals, fully fleshed out, in stiffness, thanks,
new shoes,
      smelling like a cabin of people asleep, or in your case,
scarf, coffee, skin.
           After being apart we barely talked
      on the train from the airport,
wanting to start in bed,
      not wanting to dilute beginning again
with the morning commuters.
               In this scene,
      their heads fall then bounce
awake,
      or almost awake,
then fall,
      bounce,
wake,
      or almost wake,
like a cloud trying to gather up
      its falling rain.

Freewheeling, we

set off a flock
       of starlings from
a roadside tree:
       a mess
of falling pieces
       that confuse
the road enclose
       another tree:
a same new
       form: a kind
of birth we break
       it soon enough
arriving off
       they go
from tree
       to tree
              to tree
until the road is out of trees.

Notes

Beginning Again

Elegy, for Celia

The Pyrenean ibex, or *Capra pyrenaica pyrenaica*, went extinct in 2000. A clone was born in 2009, making it the first species ever known to come back to life. The ibex kid died after seven minutes.

'Anthropocene' is commonly used to describe the present geological era, in recognition of the significant effect of our species on the earth's ecosystems. There is some debate as to when the anthropocene should be said to have begun—with the Industrial Revolution or much earlier.

Cheering the relief boat

'Hoosh': a soup made of boiled seal backbone, or whatever parts of an animal the explorers could get their hands on.

A nothing to do with God

I am indebted to C.D. O'Malley for everything here about and from Vesalius.

Painting over Aya Sofia

It turns out I was in Turkey at the same time as Mark Pashayan MD from North Carolina. After reading the poem in a journal, Mark sent me some photographs he had taken of two of the golden frescoes in Aya Sofia and one of the view over to it from the Blue Mosque. He told me nothing about himself and seemed to want nothing in return.

My line

I was helping my father move some books around his house the other day when out of the blue he said, 'You got it wrong. It is the old man walking his dog away from the camera who has the aura, not the jogger.' He wasn't angry at the mistake, nor did he take pleasure in pointing it out. He just wanted to let me know. When I checked I found he was right.

Sky, after all, meets nothing
The title is taken from Christopher Middleton's poem 'An Englishman in Texas'.
★

There are hundreds of man-made caves below the desert surface to the west
of here. Created by nuclear explosions during subterranean tests, and still
containing decaying waste, they're the hidden footnotes to the twentieth-century's
mushroom clouds. After Little Boy and Fat Man,

     Faultless, Gnome, Gasbuggy, Shoal.

Requiring of each site no water
but only rock. Rock and no water
and nobody near.

     Blasted
   ro   ck
   collapsed on

Plutonium m m m m m m m

and the burial of the clock,
nothing as lovely as
               yet with those flames no light.
Hell
urn
nature reserve
rubbish dump:

where we can't be
and are:

     Palanquin, Cabriolet, Schooner, Sulky.

Cats on Fire

Notes are included in the text.

16 Airs

Characters

Sir Aurel Stein...... (1862-1943) Archeaologist. Born in Hungary and naturalised
as a British citizen. Possessed of unwavering determination and a healthy
sense of humour. Made four major expeditions to Central Asia, bringing
back artefacts for the British Museum.

Marie...... (1922-present) Student. Appeared for the first time in T.S. Eliot's *The
Waste Land* on a sled, likely inspired by the poet's meeting with Bavarian
Countess Marie Louise Elizabeth Mendel (1858-1940). Has now fallen
on harder times. Lives on top of a honeycomb of graves in Manila,
Philippines. Spends mornings at school, afternoons scrubbing floors in a
local office block.

Sir Thomas Browne...... (1605-1682) Doctor of physic and author. Born in
London, settled in Norwich, England. Works include spiritual biography
Religio Medici; *Pseudodoxia Epidemica*, an attempt to correct popular
misconceptions of the natural world; and short history of burial practices
Urne Buriall.

The cave is woken up

Stein could not read all the perhaps 50,000 manuscripts in the 'Library Cave'. This
was partly because he had to pick through them by candlelight, in secret, since
the caretaker, Wang Yuanlu, did not want anyone to find out that he was handing
them over to a foreign explorer; and partly because Stein could not read Chinese
script. Even if he had been able to read it, he could not have known that he was
bringing back for the British Museum what is now thought to be the earliest
printed book that scholars can date with certainty (to AD 868), the Diamond
Sutra, a section of the Buddhist scriptures. The 30ft scroll has spent the last seven
years being restored.

    Stein never married, but according to his biographer Annabel Walker,
it does not appear that he was homosexual. She writes that one of his friends
suggested in a letter that he had chosen Central Asia 'for a bride'. Stein described
the remark as 'happy and delightfully true'.

A whale full of books

'Out of the head of this Whale', Browne writes, 'having been dead divers days, and under putrifaction, flowed streams of oyl and Sperma-Ceti; which was carefully taken up and preserved by the Coasters. But upon breaking up, the Magazin of Sperma-Ceti, was found in the head lying in folds and courses, in the bigness of goose eggs, encompassed with large flaxie substances, as large as a mans head, in form of hony-combs, very white and full of oyl.'

He describes the 'land of the Icthiopagi', the fish-eaters, as a place 'near the red sea, where mortars were made of the backbones of whales, doors of their jawes, & Arches of their ribbes'.

As a teenager in the north-east of England, my step-father regularly walked through a whale's jaw. It was in a park on the way from his house to the Grimsby Town football ground—and so in his mind associated with perennial disappointment.

★

In *Bookmen's Bedlam: an olio of literary oddities* (1955), Walter Hart Blumenthal begins his chapter on books bound in salvaged wood by offering his list as only the beginning of a complete one that might in the future be compiled, but which to my knowledge has not been. In his partial compilation, he mentions copies of *True Stories of HMS Royal George*, by Henry Slight, Esq., 'put in covers of that ship which was blown up in 1840 after several futile attempts to float her'; an edition of ninety copies of *Aurora Australis*, written, set, printed and bound in wood from packing cases by members of Shackleton's 1908 Antarctic expedition; and a copy of Sir Thomas Browne's *Religio Medici* bound in wood that had been floorboards of the author's house.

Some scholars have claimed that Browne willed in his last testament that his copy of Horace, 'worn out with and by me', be deposited with him in his grave. It seems, however, that these were the wishes instead of a near-contemporary of Thomas named Sir William Browne.

★

The Polynesian gods were wrapped in cloth to protect observers from their destructive power. Over time, new wrappings would have to be added as the power seeped through. Given infinite time, there might be an infinite number of layers added.

★

Schwob is Marcel, author of *Imaginary Lives*.

How they kept one another
I gave this poem one hundred and ten per cent.

Vapours
Browne believed, more or less as the ancient Greeks and Romans did, that the body is made up of four basic substances, called humours—black bile, yellow bile, phlegm and blood. Personality traits, as well as symptoms of illness, were associated with excesses and deficiencies of each humour. It was Browne's job as a physician to redress the humoural balance.

Speaking of which
One of the best-known myths about the Great Wall is of the tears of Meng Jiang. There are different versions, but usually with this basic plot.

A young woman, Meng Jiang, is separated from her husband when he is drafted by the First Emperor of the Qin dynasty (221-208 BCE) to be a labourer on the wall. At the onset of winter, she walks hundreds of miles on her own to deliver warm clothes to her husband. When she arrives, she is told that he has died of exhaustion and his bones used to build the wall that took the life from them. She cries so abundantly that the wall's foundations are loosened by tears. It collapses and her husband's bones float free.

In some versions, the story goes on. The Emperor courts Meng Jiang, who agrees to marry him on the condition that her husband is given a proper funeral. The Emperor assents. From high up on a coastal cliff, they watch the procession. Out of her mind with what she sees, the widow throws herself into the gorge, or alternatively the ocean.

★

According to Mike Davis in *Planet of Slums*, the practice of catching faeces in a plastic bag and throwing it onto the nearest roof or pathway, sometimes called a 'flying toilet', is relatively common in many slums across the so-called developing world.

His wife replies practically
        Bottled air: a business plan

Finally, the air is in the bottle:
        the smaller
smaller imprints of the same allegro fear
        of choking outsourced:

if over there that makes the stuff
        that makes the stuff
we eat gets ill from sulphur dioxide say
        the eggy one
it spoils
        the hearts while keeping them
alive for what was there before
        but communism and steppe:

the refined atmosphere here
        an imprint of almost feeling
guilt:
        for over there the spoiling air
is in the poor
        the poor is in the air: so
we are poor too?
        I mean
we must have bottled air.

Emigrants deface the caves
Around 1920, somewhere between 400 and 900 refugees who had fled the Soviet
Union after the October Revolution stayed in the caves for six months. I have not
been able to find out what happened to them after that.

        Something else I would like to find out is why some of the caves have
imitation wooden ceilings. Did wood have a religious significance? Many of the
caves were sponsored by local officials or businesspeople, and played their part in
local politics. Was it a modern, desirable look favoured by a benefactor? Unlike the
faux brick walls of the café I am sitting in now, it cannot have been intended

to fool anyone. In many cases, between the hematite rafters were painted dense honeycombs of tiny weightless Buddhas.

In several places in his travel journals Aurel Stein refers to the caves—or grottoes, or cells—as arranged in a 'honeycomb formation'. The word seems to have stuck. On a self-made blog, an American man named Rolf Gross, who 'had memorized every mountain and every wash on Stein's maps' before reaching the caves in 1983, describes them as 'honeycombing the cliff'. Unfortunately, Gross's was a 'singularly infuriating visit', since he enraged his very protective tour guide with his questions—she point-blank refused to answer those of a 'religious or iconographic nature'—and with his requests for her to hold her torch steady so he could better examine the exquisite frescoes.

In the long history of Dunhuang, the damage caused by those who passed through or found shelter in the caves is surpassed, however, by the actions of others with an entirely different purpose. As the authors of *Cave Temples of Mogao: Art and History on the Silk Road* point out, more Silk Road treasures were destroyed in seven nights of Allied bombing of Berlin in the Second World War than in the pillaging of the previous seven centuries.

Acknowledgements

I would like to acknowledge and thank the editors of the following online
and print journals and anthologies where versions of some of these poems first
appeared: *Boston Review, Cake, Clinic II, Friary House Road Editions, Geometer,
Granta, Horizon Review, IN QUIRE, Lung Jazz: Young British Poets for Oxfam,
Magma, Oxford Poetry, Poetry, Poetry London, Salt Publishing Blog, Stand*. 'Explaining
our habitats' began as a response to a painting by Alisa Henriquez; I am grateful
to H.L. Hix for pairing us. Several of these poems were also published in the
chapbook *All Safe All Well* (Flarestack Poets, 2011).

I would also like to acknowledge the support of the Arts Council UK for a
'Time to Write' grant.

Thanks to Dean Young, Brigit Pegeen Kelly, Tomaž Šalamun and Michael Adams
for encouragement and discussion early on, to Oli Hazzard for later reading, and
to David Hart and David Hawkins for conversation throughout. This book is
Daisy Hildyard's as much as it is mine.

⌐⌐ EYEWEAR PUBLISHING

EYEWEAR POETS

MORGAN HARLOW MIDWEST RITUAL BURNING
KATE NOAKES CAPE TOWN
RICHARD LAMBERT NIGHT JOURNEY
SIMON JARVIS EIGHTEEN POEMS
ELSPETH SMITH DANGEROUS CAKES
CALEB KLACES BOTTLED AIR
GEORGE ELLIOTT CLARKE ILLICIT SONNETS
HANS VAN DE WAARSENBURG THE PAST IS NEVER DEAD
DAVID SHOOK OUR OBSIDIAN TONGUES